The AI success code

A Beginner's Guide to Leveraging AI for Success in Life, Work, and Business.

By
Sophia Haves

Copyright © 2024 Sophia Haves

Disclaimer: This book is intended for educational and informational purposes only. The author is not responsible for any actions or consequences arising from the use of the information presented.

Dedication

To all those who seek to unlock their full potential,
May this book serve as a guiding light, illuminating your path to success and fulfilment.

TABLE OF CONTENT

BONUS

Real-World Applications and Industry

INTRODUCTION

Embark on an exciting exploration of artificial intelligence with "The AI Success Code." AI is reshaping our lives, making it vital to understand how to harness its power for personal and professional growth.

Through this book, we'll examine AI's evolution, key principles, and practical uses. From popular AI tools like ChatGPT to the significance of ethical AI practices, you'll discover valuable insights and strategies for integrating AI into your daily life, career, and business ventures.

As you journey through these pages, you'll uncover the secrets to:

Adopting AI at work and in your personal life

Leveraging AI for problem-solving and creativity

Harnessing AI for personal growth and development

Facing the future of AI with confidence and an ethical mindset

Let's embark on this adventure together and unlock AI's full potential. Welcome to the AI Success Code!

Part 1

How Did AI Start
A Journey Through Time

As deep learning became more prevalent in the 2010s, a new branch of AI, known as generative AI, emerged. Generative AI models focus on creating novel content, such as text, images, or audio. One groundbreaking development in generative AI was the GPT (Generative Pre-trained Transformer) model, which improved upon previous language processing techniques, allowing AI systems to produce more human-like text.

Building upon chat gpt's success, OpenAI developed ChatGPT, an advanced large language model, and released it in late 2022. ChatGPT quickly gained recognition for its remarkable ability to generate coherent, context-aware responses in diverse conversations. This language model has demonstrated potential applications in assisting users with tasks like writing, translation, and problem-solving, showcasing AI's capacity to revolutionize how we interact with technology and create content.

The advent of ChatGPT and generative AI marks an exciting milestone in AI's evolution, opening up new possibilities for human-AI interaction and content generation.

Generative AI

Unleashing the Power of Creation

In recent years, we've seen some truly amazing advancements in generative AI, which is revolutionising content creation. This technology recognizes patterns in huge datasets, resulting in diverse and unique outputs that showcase human-like creativity.

One of the most impressive things about generative AI is how it creates coherent and contextually relevant text, making AI systems feel more human. For example,

GPT and ChatGPT can engage in near-human conversations and make tasks like writing, translation, and problem-solving much easier across various industries.

Image generation has also come a long way with generative AI. Models like DALL-E 2 and Midjourney turn text prompts into stunning visuals, opening up a world of possibilities in art, design, and advertising.

Generative AI is making a significant impact across many industries, transforming the way we create and consume content.

It improves marketing strategies and enhances storytelling, offering invaluable help in scriptwriting, visual effects, and music composition for entertainment. In education, it customises learning materials, assessments, and simulations, while in healthcare, it aids medical imaging analysis, drug discovery, and patient monitoring.

As generative AI continues to evolve, its potential to reshape industries is immense, enabling personalised experiences in education and healthcare and redefining the future of content creation. The importance of generative AI cannot be overstated, and its ongoing development will undoubtedly shape the future of countless industries.

Defining AI

Key Concepts and Terminology

Let's break down some important ideas and terms related to generative AI. First off, generative AI is all about creating new data that resembles the original data it's based on. It learns the patterns and structure of the data so it can produce fresh, unique results.

You've probably heard of machine learning – it's a branch of artificial intelligence where algorithms learn from data to get better at tasks without needing specific instructions. Deep learning is a more advanced part of machine learning that uses layered neural networks. These layers let the model understand complicated patterns in the data. Neural networks, inspired by the human brain, are a bunch of algorithms working together to spot patterns. They're made up of connected nodes or neurons that process information and make predictions.

Training data is the information used to teach the AI model. It's super important because the quality and variety of this data can greatly affect how well the model performs.

One major use of generative AI is text generation, which involves creating clear and relevant text based on input data. Models like GPT and ChatGPT are great examples of this. Another application is image generation, where AI creates images from text prompts or other data. Models like DALL-E 2 and Midjourney have made some really cool progress in this area.

Hopefully, these concepts and terms give you a good understanding of how generative AI works and what it can do!

AI in the Real World

Exploring AI's Impact on Our Lives

Artificial intelligence, or AI, is all around us – it's revolutionizing industries and making our lives easier in countless ways. Let's explore some real-world examples and how AI is shaping our present and future. In healthcare, AI is a game-changer. It enables doctors to diagnose diseases more accurately and efficiently. Plus, it helps create personalized treatment plans and even contributes to medical research, speeding up drug development and potentially saving lives.

When it comes to entertainment, AI is taking center stage. It assists in creating mind-blowing special effects for movies and even helps write scripts. Not to mention, it makes recommendations for movies and TV shows based on your preferences, like having a personal entertainment guru at your service!

Transportation has seen some major transformations, too. Self-driving cars powered by AI are hitting the streets, navigating traffic, avoiding accidents, and even finding the perfect parking spots – talk about stress-free commuting!

Have you noticed how your smartphone seems to know what you're thinking? That's AI hard at work, helping tech companies create user-friendly and personalized experiences. From voice assistants like Siri and Alexa to face recognition for unlocking your phone, AI makes our lives more convenient and connected.

In finance, AI helps detect fraud, assess credit risk, and offer tailored financial advice. Online shopping has also gotten a boost from AI, with personalized product recommendations and intelligent chatbots ready to help with customer service.

The possibilities of AI are endless – from predicting natural disasters to optimizing energy consumption, it's changing the game in every field. With its vast potential to revolutionize industries and enrich our daily lives, AI is the future – and the future looks bright!

Part 2

AI Tools and Their Uses

TensorFlow: Think of this open-source library as your trusty sidekick for machine learning projects. It helps you build and train AI models for various tasks, like recognizing speech or identifying objects in images.

Scikit-learn: This toolbox is a treasure trove of algorithms and functions, making it a breeze to experiment and create AI models for tasks like grouping similar items or predicting outcomes.

PyTorch: Another handy library for deep learning, PyTorch excels in computer vision and natural language processing. It's easy to use, super-fast, and helps you build complex AI models without breaking a sweat.

Keras: A high-level neural network library, Keras simplifies the process of building AI models. It's user-friendly, works with TensorFlow, and takes care of the small details while you focus on the bigger picture.

Jupyter: Picture a virtual notebook tailored for data scientists – that's Jupyter! This web application makes it easy to write, run, and share your AI code in a convenient and interactive environment.

OpenAI Gym: Imagine a playground for AI algorithms that learn by trial and error. OpenAI Gym offers various game-like scenarios where you can train your AI models to make smarter decisions over time.

Apache Spark: Struggling with massive amounts of data? Apache Spark has your back! It's a powerful data processing engine, letting you analyse huge datasets with ease, and boosting the capabilities of AI applications.

Google Colab: A cloud-based tool perfect for AI enthusiasts, Google Colab provides a collaborative space to write, run, Thuand share AI code without worrying about technical setup.

MATLAB: This versatile tool caters to numerical computations, data analysis, and visualisation. Popular among engineers and scientists, it's used for developing AI models and tackling complex mathematical problems.

Watson: Remember IBM's famous AI system that won

Jeopardy? Watson has grown into a suite of AI tools serving various industries, from healthcare to finance. It offers top-notch natural language processing, machine learning, and data analysis capabilities.

ChatGPT

Your Trusty AI Companion for Information and Conversation

Imagine having an intelligent, ever-ready friend to chat with and explore the world of knowledge together – that's ChatGPT for you! This AI language model is designed to engage in human-like conversations, offering a remarkable experience as it answers your questions, provides information on various topics, and participates in discussions with you.

To make your interactions with ChatGPT truly delightful, keep these tips in mind:

★Ask clear and specific questions to help ChatGPT understand your queries better, allowing it to provide you with the most relevant and accurate information.

★Share context or background information when needed, so ChatGPT can offer insightful responses tailored to your needs.

★Be respectful and kind in your interactions with ChatGPT – just like any friendship, kindness goes a long way in creating a positive experience for both you and your AI companion.

ChatGPT is an amazing AI friend, eagerly waiting to chat with you and explore a wide range of topics. Go ahead, ask away! You'll soon find yourself immersed in fascinating conversations, learning new things, and building a unique bond with your AI companion.

What makes ChatGPT genuinely special is its adaptability and potential to enhance various aspects of life and industries, such as:

★**Business**: ChatGPT can assist with customer service inquiries, market research, and content generation, streamlining operations and boosting efficiency.

★**Healthcare**: AI language models like ChatGPT can help in providing personalized health advice, answering medical questions, and assisting with mental health support, contributing to improved patient care and well-being.

★**Education**: ChatGPT can serve as a valuable learning tool, answering questions, explaining complex concepts, and providing additional resources to enhance the learning experience for students of all ages.

★**Personal use:** ChatGPT can be your go-to companion for casual conversations, information seeking, and even asking for recommendations on books, movies, or hobbies, making your leisure time more enjoyable and enriching.

ChatGPT's warm and approachable nature makes it an ideal AI companion for anyone seeking information, looking for a friendly chat, or wanting to explore the numerous possibilities that AI can bring to various aspects of life and industries.

As AI technology continues to advance, we can look forward to even more sophisticated and personalized interactions with AI language models like ChatGPT. This ever-evolving journey promises exciting new experiences and opportunities for you and your AI companion to grow and learn together, transforming the way we live, work, and connect with one another.

Embrace ChatGPT with open arms, and you'll discover a loyal AI friend who's always ready to chat, help you learn, and join you on thrilling adventures through the vast world of knowledge and possibilities!

Everyday AI Tools

Boosting Productivity and Creativity

Have you ever felt like you needed a helping hand to tackle daily tasks, boost productivity, or unleash your creative side? Well, look no further than the incredible world of AI tools! These powerful resources have become an integral part of our daily lives, revolutionizing the way we work and express ourselves.

Here are some fantastic AI-powered tools that you can use to make your life easier and more creative:

Grammarly: Say goodbye to writing anxiety with this AI-driven writing assistant! Grammarly helps refine your grammar, spelling, and style, making your emails, essays, and social media posts polished and professional.

Canva: Unleash your inner artist with this user-friendly graphic design platform. Canva's AI offers design suggestions and templates for creating stunning graphics, presentations, and social media content, making it a breeze to express your ideas visually.

Spotify: Music lovers, rejoice! Spotify uses AI to curate personalised playlists based on your listening preferences, ensuring you always have the perfect soundtrack for work, play, or relaxation.

Google Translate: Break down language barriers with Google Translate, an AI-powered translation service that instantly translates text and speech across various languages.

These everyday AI tools have the power to transform your daily routine, making personal and professional tasks more manageable and creativity more accessible than ever. So go ahead and give them a try – you might just discover a whole new level of productivity and creative potential!

As AI technology continues to evolve, we can expect even more innovative tools and solutions to emerge, further enhancing our abilities and empowering us to achieve greater things in our daily lives. Embrace the possibilities that AI offers, and you'll find yourself accomplishing tasks with newfound ease and unleashing your creative genius like never before!

AI in Entertainment

Enhancing Experiences and Engagement

Have you noticed the incredible ways AI is transforming the world of entertainment? It's true — AI has become a game-changer, offering countless possibilities for enhanced experiences and engagement. Let's explore some of the amazing ways AI is revolutionizing movies, TV shows, music, and games:

Personalised Recommendations: AI-curated content ensures you spend less time browsing and more time enjoying entertainment tailored to your unique taste. Streaming platforms like Netflix and Spotify analyse your viewing and listening habits, offering suggestions that keep you entertained for hours.

Immersive Visual Effects: AI has elevated the visual effects in movies and video games, creating stunningly realistic environments that transport you to other worlds.

Interactive Storytelling: AI-driven interactive storytelling tools allow you to influence the plot, providing a truly personalised and engaging experience.

Enhanced Gaming Experiences: AI adapts game difficulty and in-game experiences based on individual player preferences and skill levels, ensuring the perfect balance of challenge and fun.

The impact of AI on the entertainment industry is undeniable, paving the way for more captivating and immersive experiences that keep us engaged and eager for more. Whether you're a movie buff, music lover, or avid gamer, prepare to embrace the AI revolution and enjoy entertainment like never before!

As AI technology progresses, we can anticipate even more exciting developments in the entertainment world, pushing boundaries and keeping us enthralled.

Part 3

AI for Business Owners
The Key to Boosting Efficiency and Unleashing Growth

Artificial intelligence (AI) has emerged as a transformative force in the business world, providing an array of opportunities to enhance efficiency and propel growth. Business owners who aim to remain competitive and optimise their operations stand to benefit significantly from AI's numerous applications. Here's a comprehensive look at how AI can revolutionise your business:

Automation: AI-powered automation is a game-changer for businesses, enabling them to streamline repetitive tasks such as data entry, scheduling, and reporting. By automating these time-consuming processes, businesses can significantly reduce human error, optimise workflow, and free up valuable resources to focus on more strategic initiatives.

Data Analysis: AI's capacity for analysing vast amounts of data is unmatched, allowing businesses to make informed, data-driven decisions. Through AI-powered analytics, companies can identify market trends, customer preferences, and areas for improvement, empowering them to stay ahead of the competition. Additionally, AI can help predict future outcomes, enabling businesses to proactively adjust strategies and capitalise on new opportunities.

Customer Service: AI has revolutionised customer service, with AI-driven chatbots and virtual assistants offering 24/7 support, personalised interactions, and faster response times. This enhanced customer experience not only improves customer retention but also attracts new customers through positive word-of-mouth and online reviews. AI also allows businesses to offer multilingual support, catering to a diverse, global customer base. Moreover, AI-powered sentiment analysis can help businesses understand customer emotions and preferences, enabling them to tailor their products and services accordingly.

Personalization: AI empowers businesses to create unique, customised experiences for each customer. By analysing customer data, AI can generate tailored product recommendations, personalized marketing messages, and custom content, fostering increased customer engagement, loyalty, and ultimately, sales. This level of personalization can lead to higher customer satisfaction, increased revenue, and long-term business success.

Sales and Marketing: AI is a powerful tool for optimising sales and marketing strategies. AI algorithms can analyse customer behaviour to identify high-value prospects, predict future purchasing behaviour, and suggest the most effective marketing channels. By automating marketing campaigns and targeting the right customers at the right time, businesses can maximise their return on investment (ROI) and drive sustainable growth.

Fraud Detection and Cybersecurity: AI plays a crucial role in safeguarding businesses from fraudulent activities and cyber threats. Machine learning algorithms can detect unusual patterns in transactions and user behaviour, flagging potential fraud cases for further investigation. In the realm of cybersecurity, AI helps identify and neutralise threats, protecting businesses' sensitive data and maintaining customer trust.

Predictive Maintenance: AI can help businesses optimise their maintenance schedules by predicting equipment failures before they occur. This proactive approach not only saves money on costly repairs but also minimises downtime, leading to more efficient operations and increased productivity.

Human Resources: AI can streamline various aspects of human resources management, from candidate screening to performance evaluations. By automating repetitive tasks and analysing employee data, AI can help businesses attract top talent, improve retention rates, and enhance overall workforce efficiency.

In the rapidly evolving business landscape, AI has become an indispensable tool for companies looking to thrive in their respective industries. By embracing AI and its wide-ranging applications, business owners can revolutionise their operations and secure long-term success.

AI in Marketing

The Secret to Personalization and Customer Engagement

Have you ever wondered how businesses manage to create such personalised marketing campaigns? The answer lies in the power of AI. AI has transformed the marketing landscape, enabling businesses to engage with their customers on a whole new level. Let's explore how AI is revolutionising marketing through personalization and customer engagement:

Personalised Content: AI analyses customer data to understand individual preferences, interests, and behaviour. This allows marketers to create highly personalised content, from customised emails to tailored product recommendations, ensuring each customer receives relevant and engaging communications.

Predictive Analytics: AI can predict future customer behaviour and preferences based on past actions and data. This predictive power allows businesses to anticipate customer needs and tailor marketing strategies accordingly, leading to more effective campaigns and increased customer satisfaction.

Chatbots and Virtual Assistants: AI-powered chatbots and virtual assistants offer 24/7 customer support, providing personalised, real-time interactions that enhance the customer experience. These tools can also gather valuable customer data to further refine marketing strategies.

Dynamic Advertising: AI enables businesses to create highly targeted ads based on customer data and behaviour. This ensures ads are displayed to the right audience at the right time, maximising ROI and fostering customer engagement.

Predictive Customer Segmentation: AI algorithms can analyse customer data to segment audiences based on shared characteristics, behaviour, and preferences. This enables businesses to create highly targeted and personalised marketing campaigns that resonate with each segment, improving overall engagement and conversion rates.

Customer Lifetime Value Prediction: AI can help businesses predict the long-term value of each customer by analysing their past behaviour and engagement patterns. This insight enables marketers to allocate resources more effectively and focus on high-value customers, maximising ROI and customer retention.

Image Recognition and Visual Search: AI-powered image recognition technology allows businesses to offer visual search capabilities, enabling customers to find products by uploading images or using their smartphone cameras. This enhances the customer experience and provides valuable data on customer preferences and trends.

Automated Campaign Optimization: AI can optimise marketing campaigns in real-time by continually analysing performance data and making adjustments based on customer responses. This ensures campaigns remain relevant and effective throughout their duration, leading to better results and higher engagement.

AI is undoubtedly the driving force behind personalised marketing experiences that engage and retain customers like never before. By leveraging AI, businesses can create meaningful connections with their audience, nurture loyalty, and ultimately drive growth.

As AI technology continues to evolve, the potential for marketing innovation is limitless. Savvy marketers who embrace AI will not only stay ahead of the competition but also unlock new opportunities for customer engagement and business success.

AI Transforming Education

A Comprehensive Approach

AI is transforming education in various ways, benefiting students, educators, and the overall learning experience. Here's a comprehensive look at how AI is revolutionising education:

Personalised Learning:

AI-powered adaptive learning platforms enable personalised experiences by tailoring content and instruction to each student's unique needs. This individualised approach improves educational outcomes and engagement.

Language Learning Tools:
AI-driven language learning tools help students acquire new language skills more effectively and efficiently. Through AI's natural language processing capabilities, these tools can provide personalised feedback, pronunciation assistance, and even simulate conversations with native speakers.

Intelligent Tutoring Systems:
AI-powered intelligent tutoring systems offer personalized instruction and guidance to students, adapting to their learning pace and providing immediate feedback. These

systems can identify knowledge gaps and provide targeted support, enhancing overall learning outcomes.

Administrative Automation: By automating administrative tasks such as grading, attendance tracking, and scheduling, AI frees up educators' time, allowing them to focus on providing quality instruction and guidance to students.

Virtual and Augmented Reality: AI-powered virtual and augmented reality technologies are increasingly used in education to create immersive learning experiences. These tools enable students to visualise complex concepts, explore historical events, or practice hands-on skills in a safe and engaging environment.

Predictive Analytics: AI can analyse student data to predict academic performance, identify at-risk students, and recommend intervention strategies. This proactive approach allows educators to provide targeted support and resources, preventing dropouts and improving overall student success rates.

Content Creation and Curation: AI can assist educators in creating and curating high-quality educational content. By analysing student data and preferences, AI can recommend relevant resources, optimise lesson plans, and even generate personalised learning materials, such as quizzes and assignments.

Inclusive Education: AI has the potential to level the playing field in education by providing accessible learning opportunities for students with disabilities or those facing geographic or socioeconomic barriers.

AI-powered assistive technologies, such as speech-to-text tools and adaptive interfaces, enable more students to participate in and benefit from education.

AI's Impact on Healthcare

A Transformation in the Making

Have you noticed how AI is revolutionizing healthcare? It's truly remarkable! Here's a rundown of how AI is changing the game in healthcare:

Improved Diagnostics: AI is like a highly skilled detective, sifting through massive amounts of medical data to help doctors diagnose conditions more accurately and swiftly. This means patients receive appropriate treatment faster, leading to better outcomes.

Preventive Care: AI excels at identifying patterns and forecasting potential health issues. By detecting problems early, healthcare providers can intervene proactively and prevent conditions from escalating.

Remote Monitoring: AI-driven wearable devices are a game-changer for healthcare! These devices monitor patients' vital signs and alert healthcare providers if something seems amiss. This enables better health management for those with chronic conditions and ensures timely medical assistance when needed.

Drug Development: AI accelerates the drug development process by quickly analyzing vast datasets to pinpoint promising treatments. This helps life-saving medications reach patients more quickly.

Administrative Efficiency: AI is a master organizer, managing tasks like appointment scheduling, medical record management, and billing. This allows doctors and nurses to focus more on patient care.

Mental Health Support:
AI-powered chatbots and virtual assistants provide round-the-clock support for people struggling with mental health issues. They offer resources, guidance, and a listening ear, promoting mental wellbeing and providing timely help.

As you can see, AI is reshaping healthcare, improving patient care, and helping people maintain their health. It's an exciting era, and it will be fascinating to watch AI's continued transformation of the healthcare landscape.

Part 4

AI Problem-Solving Hacks

Tips and Tricks for Success

Artificial intelligence (AI) can be your secret weapon when it comes to solving complex problems. Check out these incredible AI problem-solving hacks to help you tackle any challenge like a pro!

AI-Powered Data Analysis: Let AI take the heavy lifting out of data analysis by sifting through vast amounts of information and identifying patterns, trends, and insights. This will help you make informed decisions and develop tailored solutions to your problems.

Automation and Optimization: AI can automate repetitive tasks and optimise processes, saving you valuable time and resources. From customer service to supply chain management, harness the power of AI to streamline operations and boost efficiency.

Predictive Modelling: AI's predictive capabilities can help you stay one step ahead by anticipating future outcomes and trends. Use this insight to tackle problems proactively and prevent issues before they arise.

Machine Learning for Personalization: By learning from user data, AI can help you create personalised experiences that cater to individual needs and preferences. This is especially useful in fields like marketing, education, and healthcare, where a one-size-fits-all approach may not be effective.

Collaborative AI Tools: Leverage AI-driven collaboration tools to foster innovation and teamwork. These tools can facilitate communication, manage tasks, and even provide intelligent suggestions to enhance your problem-solving capabilities.

Intelligent Search and Recommendations: AI-powered search engines and recommendation systems can help you find the information and resources you need to solve problems more efficiently. From research articles to expert opinions, AI makes it easier than ever to access relevant data.

Continuous Learning: AI algorithms learn and adapt over time, improving their performance and capabilities. Embrace this spirit of continuous learning in your own problem-solving endeavours by staying open to new ideas and approaches.

By integrating AI into your problem-solving arsenal, you can unlock untapped potential and overcome even the toughest challenges. Remember, the future is AI-driven, and the possibilities are endless. Happy problem-solving with AI!

Achieving Personal Growth with AI

A Powerful Tool for Self-Improvement

Ready to tap into your full potential and achieve remarkable personal growth? Artificial intelligence (AI) can be a powerful resource in this journey. Let's explore how AI can help you become the best version of yourself:

Personalised Learning: AI-powered platforms tailor learning experiences to your individual needs, goals, and learning style. This personalised approach ensures you effectively and efficiently master new skills, propelling your personal growth.

Smart Goal Tracking: AI-driven tools help set, track, and achieve your personal growth goals. They provide data-driven insights and feedback, keeping you motivated and accountable throughout your self-improvement journey.

Habit Building and Accountability: AI assists in developing positive habits and breaking bad ones. AI-powered habit trackers and reminders keep you on top of your self-improvement game, ensuring you build sustainable routines for long-term success.

Emotional Intelligence and Mindfulness: AI-based apps and tools support emotional well-being through guided meditation, stress-reduction techniques, and mood tracking. By cultivating emotional intelligence and mindfulness, AI empowers you to face life's challenges with greater resilience and self-awareness.

Health and Fitness Optimization: AI helps you achieve optimal health and fitness with personalised workout plans, nutrition advice, and sleep tracking. By tailoring recommendations to your unique needs, AI ensures you reach your health and fitness goals safely and effectively.

Time Management and Productivity: AI-powered productivity tools streamline tasks, manage your schedule, and optimise your workflow. They keep you focused, efficient, and organised, giving you more time and energy to invest in personal growth.

Career Advancement and Networking: Leverage AI-driven platforms to expand your professional network, access mentorship opportunities, and develop new skills. AI can help you advance your career and forge meaningful connections with like-minded individuals.

Embrace the power of AI in your personal growth journey and watch your potential soar to new heights!

Embracing AI at Work

Navigating the Future with Confidence

As AI continues to shape the world of work, it's essential to adapt and embrace the opportunities it presents. Here's a guide to help you navigate the AI era with confidence:

Stay Informed: Keep up with AI advancements and their impact on your industry. Understanding the technology will help you adapt and grow alongside AI.

Upskill and Reskill: Continuously develop your skills, especially those that complement AI capabilities. Focus on building expertise in areas like critical thinking, creativity, and emotional intelligence.

Collaborate with AI: View AI as a teammate, not a rival. By working with AI tools, you can boost productivity and efficiency in your daily tasks.

Embrace Automation: Automation can handle repetitive tasks, freeing you up for more strategic and creative work. Let AI manage the routine work while you focus on high-value responsibilities.

Focus on Human Strengths: While AI excels in data processing and pattern recognition, humans bring unique skills like empathy, communication, and adaptability to the table. Highlight these strengths and leverage them in your work.

Be Adaptable: As AI technologies evolve, stay open to change and be ready to adapt your work processes accordingly. Flexibility is crucial in the AI era!

Network and Learn from Others: Connect with colleagues, industry professionals, and AI experts to share insights and learn from their experiences. Together, we can navigate the AI-driven future successfully.

Embrace the power of AI at work and confidently pave your way in the evolving professional landscape. With determination and a forward-thinking mindset, you'll be well-prepared to thrive in the age of AI.

Being Good in the Digital Age

Navigating Ethics in a Tech-Driven World

Living in a technology-driven world is exciting, but it also raises important ethical questions. How do we make sure we're doing the right thing in an era of AI, automation, and Big Data? Here's a roadmap to help you navigate ethics in our high-tech world:

Protect Privacy: In the digital age, personal data can be easily collected, stored, and shared. It's crucial to protect people's privacy by adhering to data protection regulations, seeking informed consent before collecting or sharing data, and safeguarding sensitive information from unauthorized access.

Promote Transparency: Being transparent about how technology is used can help build trust among users. Explain the benefits and risks of using a particular technology, clarify what data you collect and how it's used, and be open to addressing any concerns or questions users may have.

Mitigate Bias: Algorithms and AI systems can unintentionally perpetuate biases that exist in data or code, leading to unfair outcomes. To prevent this, it's important to use diverse and representative datasets, continuously monitor and evaluate AI models for biases, and ensure that human oversight is present in decision-making processes.

Advance Human Rights: Technology should be used to support and promote human rights, such as the right to privacy, freedom of expression, and access to information. Be mindful of how technology can impact people's lives and advocate for its responsible use.

Foster Digital Wellbeing: Digital technology can be incredibly beneficial but also overwhelming. Encourage users to develop healthy tech habits, such as setting boundaries around screen time, prioritizing meaningful connections, and seeking a balance between their online and offline lives.

Support Digital Inclusion: Bridging the digital divide is essential for ensuring everyone has equal access to technology and its benefits. This includes advocating for affordable internet access, providing digital literacy education, and ensuring that technologies are accessible to people with disabilities.

Cultivate Ethical Design: When creating new technologies, embed ethical considerations into the design process from the start. This includes evaluating potential social, cultural, and environmental impacts, as well as prioritizing user privacy, security, and wellbeing.

By considering these points and upholding ethical principles in our technology practices, we can collectively shape a more compassionate, equitable, and responsible digital world.

Part 5

The Future of AI

AI Trends and Innovations
The Future Looks Bright

The future of AI is brimming with potential, and it's no wonder there's so much excitement around it! As AI technology continues to evolve, it will bring about significant changes in various aspects of our lives. Here's a comprehensive look at some of the most promising trends and innovations that will define AI's bright future:

AI for Social Good: AI will be instrumental in tackling pressing global challenges such as climate change, healthcare, and education. By harnessing AI's predictive and analytical capabilities, we can devise innovative solutions that significantly impact people's lives and pave the way for a more sustainable world.

Explainable AI (XAI): AI systems will become more transparent and understandable, empowering users to better grasp the decision-making process. This transparency is vital for fostering trust, promoting fairness, and encouraging the ethical use of AI across diverse sectors.

Edge AI: With AI capabilities transitioning from the cloud to edge devices like smartphones and IoT gadgets, we can expect faster response times, enhanced data privacy, and a myriad of exciting new use cases. This trend will open doors for more personalised and real-time AI applications, transforming industries and improving our daily lives.

AI and the Metaverse: As AI technology integrates with the Metaverse, it will help create immersive, interactive virtual experiences that blur the lines between physical and digital worlds. AI's role in the Metaverse will revolutionise how we work, learn, play, and socialise, unlocking new possibilities for remote collaboration, immersive entertainment, and virtual learning.

AI-Powered Creativity: AI will continue to redefine the boundaries of creativity, exploring uncharted territories in arts, music, literature, and even culinary experiences. Collaborations between AI and human creators will result in groundbreaking works that redefine our understanding of creativity and innovation.

AI and Climate Change: In the fight against climate change, AI will prove to be an indispensable ally. From predicting extreme weather events and monitoring wildlife habitats to optimising energy use and identifying sustainable solutions, AI will play a pivotal role in mitigating the effects of climate change and building a greener future.

AI-Enhanced Cybersecurity: As cyber threats become increasingly sophisticated and widespread, AI will become a vital tool in detecting and responding to attacks. By utilising AI's pattern-recognition abilities, cybersecurity systems can rapidly identify and neutralise threats, fortifying our digital defences and protecting sensitive information.

As we venture into a future driven by AI, it is essential to embrace these cutting-edge trends and technologies responsibly. By cultivating a culture of ethics and collaboration between humans and AI, we can harness the full potential of AI to create a brighter, more prosperous world for all, ensuring that no one is left behind in this technological revolution.

AI and Society

How AI Is Changing Our World Artificial Intelligence (AI) has been steadily weaving its way into the fabric of our lives, revolutionising industries and shaping our society in countless ways. Let's explore the various areas where AI is making a significant impact on our world, with a special focus on its transformative role in agriculture:

Workplace Automation: AI-driven automation is rapidly changing the nature of work by taking over repetitive tasks, allowing humans to focus on more creative and strategic endeavors. This shift is reshaping job roles and creating new opportunities for those who can collaborate effectively with AI systems.

Healthcare: AI is reshaping the healthcare landscape by enabling more accurate diagnoses, personalized treatment plans, and streamlined administrative processes. AI-powered health monitoring systems can detect early warning signs of illnesses, ensuring timely interventions and better health outcomes.

Transportation: The development of AI-powered

autonomous vehicles promises to revolutionize transportation, making it safer, more accessible, and more efficient. AI-optimized traffic management systems can also reduce congestion and minimize travel times, transforming urban mobility.

Education: AI is changing the way we learn by providing personalized learning experiences and intelligent tutoring systems. These adaptive tools help students overcome learning barriers and unlock their full potential, ultimately leading to better educational outcomes.

E-commerce and Retail: AI-driven personalization algorithms are transforming online shopping experiences by offering tailored product recommendations and targeted promotions. This benefits consumers while helping retailers optimize marketing strategies and increase customer engagement.

Agriculture: AI is at the forefront of a new era in agriculture. Precision farming techniques driven by AI help farmers optimize crop yields, reduce resource waste, and improve overall efficiency. Here's a deeper look into some specific applications:

Smart Irrigation Systems: AI-driven irrigation systems monitor weather data, evapotranspiration rates, and soil moisture levels to deliver the optimal amount of water to crops. This not only conserves water but also improves crop health.

Pest and Disease Detection: AI-powered image recognition systems can detect early signs of pests and diseases, allowing farmers to intervene quickly and prevent widespread crop damage.

Predictive Analytics: AI algorithms can analyze historical data and real-time inputs to predict crop yields, market demand, and supply chain logistics, enabling farmers to optimize their operations and maximize profitability.

AI is poised to reshape our world in countless ways, with agriculture serving as just one example of its transformative power. By ensuring that AI's development and deployment are guided by ethical principles and societal values, we can harness its potential to create a more prosperous, equitable, and sustainable future for all.

Thriving in an AI-Driven Future

Skills and Strategies for Success As AI reshapes the world around us, it develops the right skills and strategies to succeed in this rapidly evolving landscape. Embracing an AI-driven future requires a unique blend of technological know-how, soft skills, and a forward-thinking mindset. Here's an in-depth look at key strategies and skills to help you navigate the dynamic world of AI:

Strategies for Success

Embrace Lifelong Learning:
With technology advancing at a rapid pace, lifelong learning is not just an option but a necessity. Stay informed about the latest AI trends, tools, and applications to remain competitive and relevant in your field.

Build a Strong Professional Network: Connect with like-minded professionals and experts in AI to exchange ideas, learn from their experiences, and stay updated on emerging trends and opportunities.

Develop a Growth Mindset: Cultivate resilience and adaptability to tackle the challenges and uncertainties of an AI-driven future. Embrace change and view obstacles as opportunities for growth and learning.

Foster Interdisciplinary Collaboration: Work closely with professionals from diverse backgrounds and disciplines to gain fresh perspectives and develop holistic solutions to complex challenges.

Participate in AI Communities and Events: Attend conferences, workshops, and webinars, and engage in online forums and communities to stay connected with the AI community and broaden your knowledge.

Skills for an AI-Driven Future

Technical Skills: Develop a solid understanding of AI concepts, programming languages, data analytics, and machine learning techniques. Proficiency in tools like Python, R, and TensorFlow will give you an advantage in the job market.

Soft Skills: Hone essential soft skills such as critical thinking, creativity, communication, and collaboration. These human-centred skills will become increasingly valuable as AI automates routine tasks and humans focus on higher-level cognitive work.

Ethical and Responsible AI: Understand the ethical implications of AI, including privacy concerns, bias, and transparency. Advocate for responsible development, deployment, and use of AI systems to ensure they benefit society as a whole.

Data Storytelling: Learn to effectively communicate data-driven insights and the impact of AI applications through compelling narratives and visuals, helping stakeholders make informed decisions.

Domain-Specific Expertise

Industry-Specific Knowledge:
Deepen your understanding of the unique AI applications and trends within your chosen industry or field. This specialised knowledge will help you identify opportunities for AI-driven innovation and growth.

Data Literacy: Strengthen your ability to interpret and analyze data, as well as communicate data-driven insights effectively. Data literacy is critical for making well-informed decisions in an AI-driven world.

Problem-Solving and Innovation: Cultivate strong problem-solving skills and a creative, innovative mindset. This will empower you to identify new use cases for AI and drive transformative change in your organisation and beyond.

By blending these strategies and skills, you'll be well-prepared to navigate the ever-evolving landscape of AI and seize the opportunities that lie ahead. Embrace the power of AI to unleash your full potential and build a brighter future for all. Remember, the key to success in an AI-driven future lies in continuous learning, adaptability, and a commitment to responsible AI practices.

The Role of AI in Sustainability and Environmental Solutions

Artificial Intelligence (AI) has emerged as a powerful tool in addressing the complex challenges of environmental sustainability. As the world grapples with issues such as climate change, resource depletion, and pollution, AI is poised to play an essential role in shaping a more sustainable future. Let's delve into how AI can contribute to various aspects of environmental sustainability:

Climate Change Mitigation and Adaptation

Energy Optimization: AI can help optimise energy systems by predicting demand, enhancing grid efficiency, and reducing waste. This results in lower greenhouse gas emissions and a more sustainable energy landscape.

Predictive Modelling: AI-powered models can forecast climate-related risks, such as extreme weather events, allowing for timely interventions and adaptation strategies.

Renewable Energy Management: AI can improve the management and integration of renewable energy sources, such as wind and solar power, into existing energy systems.

Carbon Footprint Reduction: AI can identify carbon-intensive processes and activities, providing insights to help organisations and individuals reduce their carbon footprint and combat climate change.

Natural Resource Management

Smart Agriculture: AI-driven precision agriculture techniques can optimise crop yields, reduce resource waste, and enhance land-use efficiency, promoting sustainable food production.

Water Management: AI can optimise water usage, predict droughts, and monitor water quality, enabling sustainable water resource management.

Wildlife Conservation: AI-powered image recognition

and monitoring systems can help track endangered species, detect poaching activities, and support conservation efforts.

Forestry Management: AI can help monitor forest health, detect deforestation, and predict forest fires, contributing to sustainable forestry practices.

Waste Management and Circular Economy

Smart Waste Management: AI-optimised waste collection routes and sorting systems can enhance the efficiency of waste management processes and promote recycling.

Resource Efficiency: AI can identify opportunities for resource efficiency and waste reduction across industries, fostering the transition towards a circular economy.

Recycling Optimization: AI can optimise recycling processes, improving material recovery rates and promoting the efficient use of recycled materials.

Smart Cities and Urban Planning

Intelligent Transportation Systems: AI-driven traffic management and smart public transportation solutions can reduce congestion, minimise emissions, and promote sustainable urban mobility.

Green Building Design: AI can help architects and designers optimise building designs for energy efficiency and sustainability, reducing the environmental impact of urban development.

Air Quality Monitoring: AI can monitor air quality in real-time, enabling targeted interventions to reduce pollution and improve public health.

Urban Green Space Management: AI can help identify optimal locations for urban green spaces, such as parks and green roofs, contributing to urban sustainability and livability. As AI continues to advance, its potential for driving sustainability and addressing environmental challenges will only grow. By leveraging AI's predictive, analytical, and optimization capabilities, we can develop innovative solutions that protect the environment, preserve natural resources, and build a more sustainable future for generations to come. It is crucial to ensure that AI is developed and deployed responsibly, with a focus on promoting sustainability and the well-being of both people and the planet.

Throughout this book, we've delved into the fascinating world of artificial intelligence and its potential to revolutionize industries, enhance productivity, and drive innovation. We've explored various AI applications, tools, and best practices that can help individuals and businesses harness the power of this transformative technology.

As AI continues to evolve and become more sophisticated, it's crucial for professionals and organizations to embrace this technology and adapt to the changing landscape. By doing so, they can unlock new opportunities for growth, streamline operations, and create innovative solutions to complex challenges.

To make the most of AI, remember to invest in the necessary resources, foster a culture of innovation, and continuously learn and experiment with new tools and techniques. By staying informed and proactive, you'll be well-equipped to navigate the exciting world of artificial intelligence and achieve success in an increasingly AI-driven future.

In closing, the key to realizing the full potential of AI lies in understanding its capabilities, addressing its limitations, and leveraging it responsibly to create meaningful solutions that benefit society. As we move forward, let's continue exploring the incredible possibilities of AI and work together to build a brighter, more innovative future.

Bonus Topic

Tech Trends

Introduction

The Importance of Keeping Up with Technology Trends

In today's fast-paced world, technology continues to rapidly evolve, impacting every aspect of our lives and shaping the future of various industries. From artificial intelligence to blockchain, the advancements in technology are not only changing how we live and work but also redefining the way businesses operate and compete.

Keeping up with technology trends is essential for several reasons:

Competitive Advantage: Businesses that stay ahead of the curve in adopting and implementing emerging technologies are better positioned to gain a competitive edge in their respective industries. Embracing new technologies can lead to increased efficiency, reduced costs, and the development of innovative products and services.

Career Growth: For professionals, staying informed about the latest technology trends can help identify new opportunities for career growth and skill development. Understanding how emerging technologies are shaping the job market can give individuals a competitive advantage in the workforce.

Informed Decision-Making: Being aware of the potential impact of emerging technologies enables individuals and organisations to make more informed decisions, whether it's investing in new products, adopting new business strategies, or pursuing further education.

Societal Impact: Technology has the power to reshape society, and staying informed about emerging trends allows individuals to engage in meaningful conversations about the ethical and societal implications of new technologies.

In this bonus section, we'll explore the latest technology trends and their real-world applications, discuss future predictions, and offer tips on how to stay ahead in a rapidly evolving tech landscape. By keeping up with technology trends, you'll be better equipped to navigate the challenges and seize the opportunities presented by the ever-changing world of technology.

Latest Technology Trends

The world of technology continues to advance at breakneck speed, bringing forth a variety of trends that are transforming the way we live and work. Here are some of the latest technology trends shaping our world today:

1.Artificial Intelligence (AI)

Artificial Intelligence (AI) has become a driving force behind many technological advancements, with the ability to simulate human intelligence in machines. This has led to significant improvements in various industries, as AI can perform tasks that previously required human intervention. Some key developments in AI include:

Machine Learning: Algorithms that enable machines to learn from data, identify patterns, and make predictions without explicit programming.

Natural Language Processing: Technology that enables machines to understand, generate, and process human language, enabling more natural communication between humans and machines.

Deep Learning: A subset of machine learning that uses artificial neural networks to solve complex problems, such as image and speech recognition.

Robotics: The integration of AI and robotics has led to the development of intelligent machines capable of performing tasks in manufacturing, logistics, healthcare, and other sectors.

Autonomous Systems: AI is powering the development of autonomous vehicles, drones, and other systems that can navigate and operate independently, transforming transportation and logistics.

2.Blockchain

Blockchain technology has transcended its initial association with cryptocurrencies like Bitcoin, demonstrating its potential for applications across various industries. At its core, blockchain is a decentralised, tamper-proof ledger that enables secure, transparent, and efficient transactions. Some of the key features and applications of blockchain include:

Decentralisation: Blockchain operates on a peer-to-peer network, eliminating the need for intermediaries like banks or governments.

Immutability: Once a transaction is recorded on the blockchain, it cannot be altered, ensuring transparency and trust.

Smart Contracts: These self-executing contracts automatically enforce the terms of an agreement when specific conditions are met, streamlining processes and reducing the need for intermediaries.

Supply Chain Management:
Blockchain can help track goods,
monitor conditions, and ensure
authenticity, promoting
transparency and efficiency in
supply chains.

Financial Services: Blockchain
enables faster, more secure, and
cost-effective financial
transactions, including
cross-border payments,
remittances, and trade finance.

3.Cybersecurity

With the growing dependence on digital technologies, cybersecurity has become a top priority for individuals, businesses, and governments alike. The rapid expansion of the internet and the proliferation of connected devices have created new opportunities for cybercriminals and hackers, necessitating constant innovation in cybersecurity solutions. Some key aspects of cybersecurity include:

Threat Detection and Prevention: Tools and techniques designed to identify and neutralise potential threats before they cause harm.

Encryption: The process of encoding data to ensure that only authorised parties can access it, protecting sensitive information from unauthorised access.

Identity and Access Management: Ensuring that only authorised individuals can access specific resources and data within an organisation.

Incident Response: The process of responding to and recovering from security breaches, minimising damage and preventing future incidents.

Cybersecurity Awareness: Educating individuals and organisations about potential risks and best practices for maintaining a strong cybersecurity posture.

As cyber threats continue to evolve, the need for robust and proactive cybersecurity measures will remain critical for safeguarding digital assets and infrastructure.

4.Internet of Things (IoT)

Imagine a world where everyday objects, from your refrigerator to your car, are connected to the internet and can communicate with one another. This is the world of the Internet of Things (IoT), a rapidly growing network of interconnected devices that are making our lives smarter, more efficient, and more convenient.

The Internet of Things has various applications across different industries, including:

Smart Homes: IoT-enabled devices like thermostats, lighting systems, and security cameras can be remotely controlled and monitored, making our homes more comfortable and secure.

Healthcare: Remote patient monitoring, smart medical devices, and smart hospitals are revolutionizing patient care and improving healthcare outcomes.

Manufacturing: Industrial IoT is optimizing production processes, improving efficiency, and reducing downtime through predictive maintenance and real-time monitoring.

Transportation: Connected cars, smart traffic management systems, and autonomous vehicles are transforming the way we travel and commute.

Agriculture: IoT sensors and systems can monitor crop health, soil conditions, and water usage, enabling more sustainable and efficient farming practices.

As the Internet of Things continues to expand, we can expect even more innovation and transformation in our daily lives and across various industries. However, it is essential to address potential challenges such as data privacy, security, and interoperability to fully realize the benefits of this connected world.

4.Augmented Reality (AR) and Virtual Reality (VR)

We live in an exciting time when the lines between the physical and digital worlds are blurring, thanks to Augmented Reality (AR) and Virtual Reality (VR). These cutting-edge technologies are changing how we interact with our surroundings, creating new possibilities for entertainment, education, and work.

Augmented Reality (AR) superimposes digital information onto the real world, enhancing our perception and interaction with our environment. Some popular applications of AR include:

Gaming: Mobile games like Pokémon Go have popularised AR by blending virtual characters with the real world.

Retail: Virtual try-on features and in-store navigation help shoppers visualise products and enhance their shopping experience.

Education: AR brings learning to life by overlaying digital information on textbooks, maps, and other educational materials.

Virtual Reality (VR), on the other hand, immerses users in a completely digital environment, offering a fully immersive experience. Some applications of VR include:

Gaming: VR headsets like Oculus Rift and PlayStation VR enable gamers to experience virtual worlds in a whole new dimension.

Training: From flight simulations to medical procedures, VR provides a safe and realistic environment for hands-on training.

Tourism: Virtual tours of museums, historical sites, and even outer space allow users to explore new destinations from the comfort of their homes.

As AR and VR technologies continue to evolve and become more accessible, we can expect even more innovative applications that redefine our perception of reality and reshape how we live, learn, and play.

Success Stories

Real-World Applications and Industry Disruptors

As technology continues to evolve, we witness innovative ideas transforming into groundbreaking solutions that reshape industries and redefine how we live, work, and interact with the world. Let's explore a few success stories that showcase the real-world impact of emerging technologies:

Airbnb: By leveraging the sharing economy and digital platforms, Airbnb has revolutionized the travel and hospitality industry, offering unique accommodations and experiences for travelers worldwide.

Tesla: With a focus on electric vehicles, autonomous driving, and renewable energy, Tesla is driving innovation in the automotive industry while paving the way for a more sustainable future.

Stripe: By building a powerful and user-friendly payment processing platform, Stripe has become a leading player in the fintech industry, enabling businesses of all sizes to accept payments online and scale their operations.

Zoom: As remote work and virtual collaboration become increasingly prevalent, Zoom's video conferencing platform has emerged as a vital tool for businesses, educational institutions, and individuals, connecting people across the globe.

Amazon Web Services (AWS): AWS has transformed the cloud computing landscape by providing scalable, reliable, and cost-effective cloud services, empowering organisations to accelerate their digital transformation efforts.

These industry disruptors demonstrate the power of leveraging emerging technologies to create innovative solutions and drive positive change. As new technologies continue to emerge, we can expect even more groundbreaking success stories that reshape industries and redefine the way we live and work.

Future Predictions
Emerging Technologies and Their Impact

As we look ahead, emerging technologies will continue to shape our world and transform industries. Here are some predictions for the future impact of these technologies:

AI and Automation: Widespread adoption of AI and automation will redefine the job market, requiring new skill sets and creating opportunities for innovation.

Blockchain: Blockchain will revolutionise industries like finance, supply chain, and healthcare, enabling secure, transparent, and decentralised transactions.

5G Networks: 5G networks will drive advancements in IoT, AR/VR, and smart city infrastructure, enhancing connectivity and data transfer speeds.

Quantum Computing: Quantum computers will solve complex problems, accelerating advancements in fields like drug discovery, climate modelling, and cryptography.

Edge Computing: Edge computing will support real-time data processing, enabling smart devices and IoT systems to operate more efficiently and securely.

As these technologies continue to evolve and converge, we can expect even more transformative changes that will shape the future of businesses and society.

Growth of Smart Cities

As urban populations continue to grow, smart cities will play a crucial role in managing resources, improving public services, and enhancing the quality of life for residents. Key aspects of smart city development include:

IoT Integration: IoT sensors and devices will monitor and manage city infrastructure, including transportation, utilities, and public services.

Data Analytics: Data-driven decision-making will enable city officials to allocate resources more efficiently and develop targeted solutions to urban challenges.

Connectivity: High-speed networks like 5G will support communication between IoT devices and provide reliable internet access for residents.

Sustainable Development: Smart cities will prioritise green spaces, energy-efficient buildings, and sustainable transportation solutions.

Citizen Engagement: Digital platforms and mobile apps will empower citizens to access public services, report issues, and participate in city planning.

As more cities embrace smart technologies, we can expect urban environments to become more livable, sustainable, and responsive to the needs of their residents.

Tips for Staying Ahead
Adapting and Thriving in a Rapidly Evolving Tech Landscape

To stay ahead in the ever-changing world of technology, consider the following strategies:

Embrace Lifelong Learning: Continuously update your skills and knowledge through online courses, workshops, and industry events.

Monitor Industry Trends: Stay informed about emerging

technologies and their potential impact on your industry.

Network with Industry Peers: Connect with professionals in your field to share insights and learn from their experiences.

Foster a Growth Mindset: Be open to new ideas and approaches, embracing change as an opportunity for growth and innovation.

Experiment and Innovate: Test new technologies and explore creative solutions to industry challenges.

As we've explored throughout this book, technology continues to evolve at an unprecedented pace, reshaping industries and transforming our world in profound ways. From artificial intelligence and blockchain to the growth of smart cities, the advancements we've discussed are not only changing the way we live and work but also presenting new opportunities for innovation and growth.

To stay ahead in this rapidly evolving landscape, it's essential to embrace lifelong learning, monitor industry trends, and foster a growth mindset that views change as an opportunity rather than a challenge. By doing so, you'll be well-prepared to navigate the ever-changing world of technology and seize the opportunities presented by emerging tech trends.

Ultimately, the future of technology is filled with endless possibilities, and those who stay informed and adaptable will be best positioned to thrive in an increasingly connected, data-driven, and innovative world. So, as we look ahead to the future of technology, remember to stay curious, embrace change, and continue exploring the incredible potential of emerging tech trends.

A Message of Appreciation

As we come to the end of this journey through the AI Success Code, I want to take a moment to express my heartfelt gratitude to you, the reader. Your dedication to learning and exploring the vast potential of artificial intelligence is truly inspiring, and I hope this book has provided valuable insights and tools to help you achieve success in this exciting field.

I want to extend my sincere appreciation to everyone who contributed to making this book a reality, including industry experts, researchers, and the countless innovators pushing the boundaries of AI. Your insights, experiences, and passion for this transformative technology have helped shape this book into an essential guide for those seeking to harness the power of AI.

To my publisher, collaborators, and editors, thank you for your unwavering support and guidance throughout this process. Your expertise and commitment have been invaluable in bringing this book to fruition.

Finally, to my readers, thank you for joining me on this journey through the AI Success Code. I am honoured to have shared my knowledge and experiences with you and look forward to witnessing the incredible advancements you'll make in the world of artificial intelligence. Together, let's continue to explore, learn, and innovate as we shape a brighter future powered by AI.

With heartfelt appreciation,

Sophia Haves.

www.ingramcontent.com/pod-product-compliance
Lightning Source LLC
LaVergne TN
LVHW051342050326
832903LV00031B/3684